21st
Century
Skills Library

COOL SCIENCE CAREERS

FOOD SCIENTIST

BARBARA A. SOMERVILL

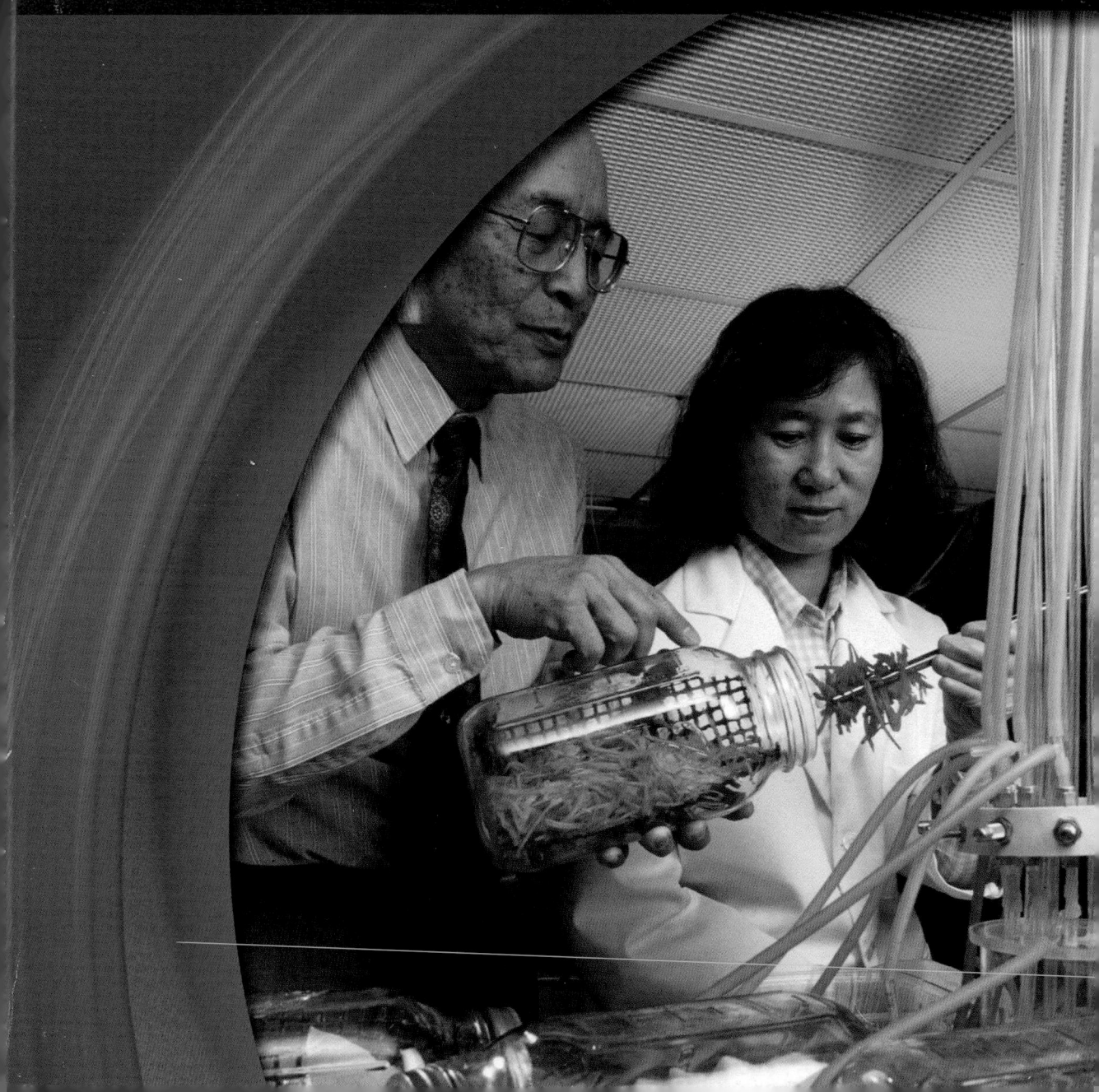

Published in the United States of America by
Cherry Lake Publishing, Ann Arbor, Michigan
www.cherrylakepublishing.com

Content Adviser
Michele Perchonok, PhD, Member Expert, Institute of Food Technologists

Credits
Photos: Cover and pages 1 and 22, Photo courtesy of Scott Bauer, USDA Agricultural
Research Service; page 4, Photo courtesy of Jean Guard-Petter, USDA Agricultural
Research Service; page 7, ©AGStockUSA, Inc./Alamy; page 9, ©ClassicStock/Alamy;
page 10, iStockphoto.com/RapidEye; page 11, ©Nigel Cattlin/Alamy; page 12,
©ARCTIC IMAGES/Alamy; page 15, ©H. Mark Weidman Photography/Alamy;
page 16, ©ImageDJ/Alamy; page 19, ©Johanna Goodyear, used under license from
Shutterstock, Inc.; pages 20 and 24, ©Jim West/Alamy; page 23, Photo courtesy of
Stephen Ausmus, USDA Agricultural Research Service; page 26, Photo courtesy of
Keith Weller, USDA Agricultural Research Service; page 28, Photo courtesy of Bruce
Fritz, USDA Agricultural Research Service

Library of Congress Cataloging-in-Publication Data
Somervill, Barbara A.
  Food scientist / by Barbara A. Somervill.
     p. cm.—(Cool science careers)
  Includes index.
  ISBN-13: 978-1-60279-505-1
  ISBN-10: 1-60279-505-3
  1. Food—Research—Vocational guidance—Juvenile literature. I. Title.
II. Series.
  TX355.S6485 2009
  664.0023—dc22   2008044183

Cherry Lake Publishing would like to acknowledge
the work of The Partnership for 21st Century Skills.
Please visit *www.21stcenturyskills.org* for more information.

TABLE OF CONTENTS

CHAPTER ONE
WHAT'S ON YOUR TABLE? 4

CHAPTER TWO
**THE WORLD OF FOOD
  SCIENCE** 12

CHAPTER THREE
**BECOMING A FOOD
  SCIENTIST** 20

CHAPTER FOUR
**A FUTURE IN FOOD
  SCIENCE** 24

SOME FAMOUS FOOD SCIENTISTS 29
GLOSSARY 30
FOR MORE INFORMATION 31
INDEX .32
ABOUT THE AUTHOR 32

CHAPTER ONE
WHAT'S ON YOUR TABLE?

You sit down to a dinner of roasted chicken, mashed potatoes, green beans, and a glass of milk. You might not think: Is this food safe to eat? You probably trust that your

Food scientists study colonies of bacteria that can infect food, such as this colony of Salmonella enteritidis.

food has been handled carefully from the farm to the store to your home. Who helps make that happen? Food scientists play a big role.

Picture that chicken dinner. Workers from the United States Department of Agriculture (USDA) inspected the chicken farm and processing plant. The vegetables were kept fresh at the grocery store. The milk was refrigerated to keep it from spoiling. Throughout North America, food scientists work to make sure that you have food that is safe to eat.

Food science combines chemistry, biology, agriculture, **economics**, **engineering**, and cooking. In laboratories, food scientists develop and test every ingredient that is added to food. They study **bacteria** that grow in food and might cause illnesses, such as *Salmonella*. Food scientists research ways to grow crops that yield more grain or vegetables. They also study ways to grow food with higher vitamin or mineral levels. They study ways to process, package, label, and ship food products. They also develop new products, such as breakfast cereals and peanuts that don't contain allergens.

Food science is a fairly young field of study. In the late 1800s, people who processed, packaged, or sold food had few laws they had to follow. Some companies produced and sold food that made people sick. That changed when Dr. Harvey Wiley joined the USDA in 1883. Wiley saw three big problems with the U.S. food supply. First, there were no laws to stop people from adding strange substances to food. Second, many of the food products sold to the public were not properly labeled. And third, companies used false advertising to sell their food products.

21ST CENTURY CONTENT

Peanuts are an important source of protein. They can be grown in many countries and feed hungry people. They contain important vitamins and healthy fats. Many people, however, are **allergic** to peanuts. Food scientists are working to find a solution to peanut allergies. They've developed a way to remove the substances in peanuts that cause allergic reactions. This process will allow more people to eat peanuts.

Are you allergic to peanuts? Finding out how to manage your allergies is an important part of staying healthy. The Internet can be a great resource. Check out *kidshealth.org/kid/ stay_healthy/food/nut_allergy.html* for more information on peanut allergies.

In 1884, Wiley and several other chemists formed the Association of Official Agricultural Chemists. This group began testing U.S. foods and found some frightening results.

A farmer holds freshly harvested peanuts.

For example, tea companies were selling tea leaves contaminated with high levels of chemicals such as arsenic and lead. Wiley used the results from food science tests to convince Congress to pass food safety laws. These laws affected dairy products, spices, candy, tea, coffee, cereal, meat, and other products. The laws made U.S. foods safer.

In the 1900s, large food companies emerged. They hired food scientists to develop more products for grocery store shelves. Breakfast cereals were totally new products. Shoppers bought wheat flakes, cornflakes, and shredded wheat.

The 1930s saw another change in how Americans bought and stored food. The electric refrigerator allowed people to store cold foods. This meant fewer trips to the supermarket. Food scientists developed more refrigerated products. They also worked on ways to package and ship those products.

By the 1950s, shoppers wanted more than just basic ingredients on supermarket shelves. Many men who had served in the military in World War II had been stationed in Europe and Asia. After soldiers returned home, they wanted to keep eating lasagna and other **ethnic** foods.

Food scientists developed hundreds of products to meet the growing demand for ethnic foods. These products included different shapes of pasta, canned pasta sauces, different types of bread, canned Mexican salsas, and even Chinese stir-fry. Homemakers also wanted convenience. Food scientists came up with a wider variety of frozen foods and TV dinners.

A salesman demonstrates a refrigerator to a customer in the 1930s. Food scientists developed many refrigerated products after the electric refrigerator was invented.

The next food trend involved health and food safety. Americans looked to the U.S. government to tightly control food quality and content. Food scientists led the fight for better nutritional labeling and product standards. People also wanted to eat healthier and have foods with reduced fats and sugar. These trends have kept food scientists busy.

Look at the milk for sale in your supermarket. Milk products include whole, skim, 2%, 1%, chocolate, and others. Milk is sold in plastic jugs and cardboard containers in a variety of sizes. Milk is refrigerated at a temperature below 40 degrees Fahrenheit (4.4 degrees Celsius). Most milk has

Grocery stores have many different milk products for sale.

This stainless steel equipment is used to pasteurize milk.

vitamins A and D added. This fact is clearly labeled. Nutrition information is printed clearly on the package. So is the date that the milk must be sold by. The milk is **pasteurized** to reduce bacteria. Food science truly has followed the milk you drink from the cow to your refrigerator.

CHAPTER TWO
THE WORLD OF FOOD SCIENCE

Food scientists have jobs in laboratories, factories, at colleges, or on farms. They can work for big corporations, the government, or the military. They can also have their own private businesses.

Food scientists perform tests on fish in a laboratory.

In 2006, about 14 percent of food scientists in the United States worked for the government. Nearly 20 percent taught at colleges or universities. The rest worked for a variety of companies. These companies ranged from seed producers and chocolate makers to dairy processors and fast-food restaurants.

LEARNING & INNOVATION SKILLS

Research and development is big business for food scientists. During the development process, food scientists must ask themselves many questions. What will the product be made of? How will it be made? What nutritional value will it have? How can it be packaged? What flavors should the product be available in? Asking questions leads food scientists toward solutions. They might create a dozen different samples. The samples are tested for flavor, quality, and appearance. Taste tests help determine which sample will sell best. Can you think of more questions that food scientists might ask as they come up with new products?

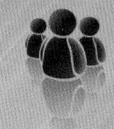

LIFE & CAREER SKILLS

In 1986, food scientist Norman Borlaug founded the World Food Prize. This prize honors scientists and other experts who work to improve the world's food supply. The public may not be aware of many of these men and women, but their efforts help feed billions of hungry people. Philip E. Nelson, a food scientist, won the prize in 2007. His work has led to better ways of storing and transporting large amounts of fresh food around the world. Some winners have developed high-yield rice or high-protein maize.

The World Food Prize is a very special award. It recognizes people such as food scientists who were determined to become not only experts, but true leaders in their field. Through their hard work and commitment, they've made a difference in the world.

What do all of these food scientists do at work? Food scientists who work for food companies often do "cuttings." A cutting is a test of a final product for quality. What would a cutting of blueberry yogurt involve? Let's say a company produces 25,000 cups of yogurt per day. A food scientist pulls

Food manufacturers must perform quality control checks on their products.

some samples of finished yogurt from the production line. The sample is checked for color, texture, and taste. Yogurt has live bacteria in it. The bacteria levels are checked. The yogurt must be tested to make sure it does not contain any foreign matter, such as a blueberry stem. Throughout the world, food scientists do cuttings on thousands of products every day.

Some food scientists work to find ways to produce better varieties of grains such as wheat.

Food scientists who work at colleges can be teachers. They can also do research to develop new varieties of grains, fruits, and vegetables. They look for ways to produce more food. They also work to produce higher-quality, more nutritious food.

Sometimes food becomes tainted. If people eat that food, they may get sick. Have you ever heard of food poisoning? That is just one of many different types of food-related illnesses. Some are more serious than others. *Salmonella* is caused by bacteria. It is the most commonly reported foodborne illness. Other common foodborne illnesses involve *E. coli* or other bacteria.

In the United States, 76 million people get sick from illnesses related to tainted food every year. Most of these people think they just have an upset stomach. Around 5,000 of these people die. When an outbreak of foodborne illness is reported, food scientists become detectives. They must find the cause of the illness and figure out how to prevent more people from getting sick.

Mad cow disease is a deadly disease that kills cows by attacking the nervous system. This disease threatened the cattle industry in the late 1990s. In Europe, some people became sick from eating infected meat. Many people refused to buy beef out of fear that it might carry the protein that caused mad cow disease. That protein can also cause human deaths.

21ST CENTURY CONTENT

Bacteria can contaminate food at any point during production or processing. Storing foods correctly is one basic food safety rule. Keep hot foods hot and cold foods cold. People who handle foods should wash their hands frequently. What are some other steps people can take to help prevent food poisoning?

In 2007, scientists found a way to breed cattle that cannot catch mad cow disease. The process for producing these cows is called genetic engineering. A genetically modified food is one that has had its **genes** changed in some way. The idea of altering the genes in food to create new, better products bothers some people. They worry about whether genetically engineered food is safe to eat. Others argue that these foods could be a tool used to fight world hunger. The discussion will continue in the years to come.

Some food scientists work to make sure cattle are free from diseases such as mad cow disease.

CHAPTER THREE

BECOMING A FOOD SCIENTIST

What kind of training do you need if you want to be a food scientist? In high school, students who want to pursue a science career should take biology, chemistry, and physics. Basic courses in using computers and in economics will also build useful skills.

Studying chemistry is important if you want to become a food scientist.

Becoming a food scientist requires a college degree. The amount of education needed depends on the type of work a food scientist wants to do. Food scientists study chemistry, biology, **microbiology**, **biochemistry**, engineering, and mathematics. Those who wish to work directly in food production may need special courses in agricultural science.

LEARNING & INNOVATION SKILLS

NASA has a team of food scientists working with other experts to develop menus for astronauts. They must think creatively to overcome the challenges of eating in space. For example, you can't sprinkle salt and pepper in space. Why not? Salt and pepper would float and might go up an astronaut's nose! That's why food scientists developed liquid salt and pepper. Tortillas are used because they make fewer crumbs and take up less storage space than bread. By thinking creatively, scientists are able to provide a greater variety of food for astronauts.

Many students who earn bachelor of science (BS) degrees in food science complete an internship as part of their course work. Interns get hands-on job experience by being student workers in their field of interest. Some interns might work at food processing plants or in government laboratories. Sometimes students are paid for the work they do as interns. But some just work to earn valuable experience. Most students find that it is easier to get a job if they have worked as an intern.

A college graduate with a BS degree starts off with an entry-level or basic food science job. This might involve **quality assurance**, sales, or product development.

Food scientists need to learn how to use many different kinds of lab equipment.

Many food scientists work outside of labs, helping farmers grow healthy, nutritious crops.

Some food scientists continue their studies and get a master's degree or a doctorate. Food scientists with master's degrees may be managers of product development, microbiology labs, or quality assurance labs. Food scientists with doctorates often work as college professors or research scientists.

CHAPTER FOUR
A FUTURE IN FOOD SCIENCE

The outlook for food science jobs is good. Over the past 50 years, food scientists have developed exciting food products. Some of them are microwavable meals, quick-cooking frozen foods, pudding cups, low-fat and low-sugar

Some scientists worry that the use of crops to produce biofuel will worsen the hunger problem in poor countries.

ice cream, and many snacks. The future will bring even more new products.

Today's food scientists also face global problems. These include pollution, terrorism, and **biofuel** demands. They look for solutions to the problems of an uneven food supply. The world struggles with hunger in some countries and obesity from overeating in others.

LEARNING & INNOVATION SKILLS

Today, corn and soybean plants are used to create biofuel for cars and trucks. But many food scientists think that feeding the hungry with those plants is more important than using it for fuel. They argue that we should look for other fuel sources. They say that corn and soybeans should be used to feed starving people. It is possible to make biofuel from other products, such as switchgrass, algae, or recycled frying oil.

Finding better solutions to energy and food problems is complex. Scientists must consider all the ways a new fuel can affect people, wildlife, and the environment. What do you think? Should people stop producing fuel from corn and soybeans?

Pollution affects our food supply in many ways. Chemical pollution from factories, automobiles, and even jets is found in water and the air. Pollution enters plants and crops through rain and soil. It enters animals through water and feed. Reducing pollution levels would make the food we eat safer.

Food terrorism involves people adding biological or chemical substances to food on purpose. These substances make people sick. The U.S. government believes terrorists may threaten food safety. Possible terrorist acts could include poisoning food products with *E. coli*, *Salmonella*, or the bacteria that causes anthrax. *E. coli* and *Salmonella* make people sick

A food scientist examines a tomato that is part of a genetic engineering research project.

to their stomachs and give them diarrhea. Anthrax is a disease that can be deadly. Food scientists create safe packaging and testing methods to reduce the possibility of food terrorism.

Two exciting fields in food science that require special training are **biotechnology** and **nanotechnology**. These fields use the newest technology to solve food science problems.

One aspect of biotechnology involves changing the basic genetics of plants and crops. These changes make plants stronger or help them resist drought or extreme cold. Biotechnology has been used to produce larger or more tomatoes, rice, and potatoes.

Bioengineered foods worry some people. They fear that foods made by changing the genetic makeup of grains will not be safe to eat. Believe it or not, scientists have been working with plant and animal genetics for more than 100 years. Certain potatoes, tomatoes, and grapefruits are "engineered" products we eat all the time.

About 70 percent of processed foods in North American supermarkets are made from genetically engineered plants. Nearly all breads, cakes, cookies, breakfast cereals, frozen pizzas, pasta, and soda contain some type of bioengineered ingredient.

Some food scientists research and develop biotech food products. Other food scientists test them for safety. The U.S. Food and Drug Administration (FDA) has tested more than 50 biotech food products and found them safe to eat. These products include canola oil, corn, potatoes, soybeans, squash, sugar beets, and tomatoes.

Nanotechnology involves moving very tiny particles to make new materials or products. Scientists use special microscopes and tools to help them do this. Food scientists apply nanotechnology to new foods, packaging, and nutrition products, such as multivitamins. Here's an example of nano-technology at work: silver and minerals can be added to the plastic in food containers to keep fish, fruit, and other products fresher longer.

Food science is a growing, changing, exciting area of study. Food scientists work in factories, labs, and fields. They can work for private companies or the government. No matter what job a food scientist has, the goals are always the same. Food scientists want to produce more good-quality, nutritious food.

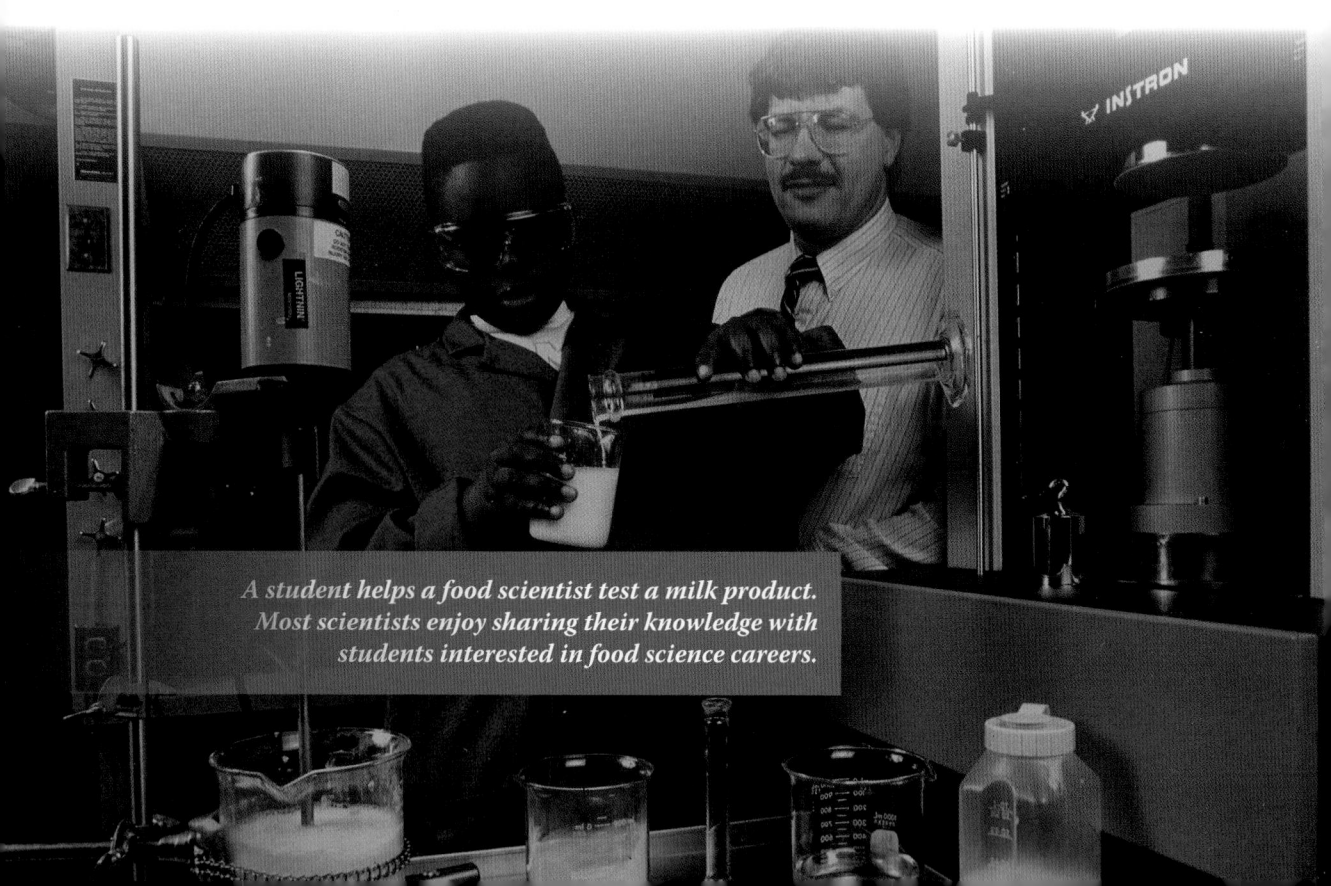

A student helps a food scientist test a milk product. Most scientists enjoy sharing their knowledge with students interested in food science careers.

SOME FAMOUS FOOD SCIENTISTS

Clarence Birdseye (1886–1956) revolutionized how food was processed when he developed a way to freeze and package fish and vegetables. This process allowed fresh foods to be frozen for later use. It was a breakthrough that changed the food industry.

Dr. Norman Borlaug (1914–) developed high-yield wheat. In 1970, he won the Nobel Peace Prize for his work to reduce world hunger. He also founded the World Food Prize. This award honors food people who work to find better ways to feed hungry people.

Dr. Philip E. Nelson (1934–) is a U.S. food scientist who developed important techniques for storing and transporting fresh foods. Large amounts of food could be shipped around the world without losing its taste or nutrients. He was awarded the World Food Prize in 2007.

Dr. Michele Perchonok (1955–) is a leading food scientist at NASA's Johnson Space Center in Houston, Texas. Her job is to develop ways of processing, packaging, and producing food for astronauts as they travel through space.

Dr. Nevin S. Scrimshaw (1918–) has devoted a lifetime to relieving malnutrition in developing nations. He developed Incaparina, a special mixture of cottonseed flour and maize. High in protein and inexpensive to make, Incaparina is fed to thousands of infants in Guatemala to fight disease caused by low-protein diets. Dr. Scrimshaw also developed Balahar from peanut flour and wheat. It helped people cope with famine in India.

GLOSSARY

allergic (uh-LUR-jik) having or related to a condition in which the body has an abnormal reaction after contact with a substance

bacteria (bak-TIHR-ee-uh) small, one-celled organisms

biochemistry (bye-oh-KEM-is-tree) the study of the chemistry of living things

biofuel (BYE-oh-fyool) fuel produced from plant matter

biotechnology (bye-oh-tek-NOL-uh-jee) the use of living things or biological processes to make products

economics (ek-uh-NOM-iks) the study of the production, distribution, and purchase of goods and services

engineering (en-juh-NEER-ing) the application of scientific, mathematical, and technological knowledge to practical human needs

ethnic (ETH-nik) having to do with a specific culture or nationality

genes (JEENS) tiny building blocks of all living things, they are passed from parent to offspring and determine how a living thing looks and grows

microbiology (mye-kroh-bye-OL-uh-jee) the study of microscopic organisms

nanotechnology (na-noh-tek-NOL-uh-jee) the use of atoms and molecules to create new products

pasteurized (PASS-chuh-rized) heated enough to kill bacteria and other microscopic organisms without changing the taste or nutritional value of the food

quality assurance (KWAHL-uh-tee uh-SHUR-uhnss) a system for checking and evaluating a product to make sure it meets certain standards

FOR MORE INFORMATION

BOOKS

Franchino, Vicky. *Genetically Modified Foods*. Ann Arbor, MI: Cherry Lake Publishing, 2008.

Graham, Ian. *Food Technology*. Mankato, MN: Black Rabbit Books, 2009.

Miller, Jeanne. *Food Science*. Minneapolis: Lerner Publications, 2009.

WEB SITES

Bureau of Labor Statistics: Agricultural and Food Scientists
www.bls.gov/oco/ocos046.htm
Discover lots of information about what food scientists do

NASA: Michele Perchonok, Shuttle Food System Manager
www.nasa.gov/audience/foreducators/stseducation/stories/Michele_Perchonok_Profile.html
Learn more about what astronauts eat and the work of NASA food scientists

The World Food Prize: About the Prize
www.worldfoodprize.org/about/about.htm
Find out more about this special award

21ST CENTURY SKILLS LIBRARY

INDEX

astronauts, 21, 29

bacteria, 5, 10, 16,
    17, 26
biotechnology, 27
Birdseye, Clarence, 29
Borlaug, Norman, 14,
    29

contamination, 7–8,
    17

development, 5,
    6, 8–9, 13, 14,
    16–17, 21, 22,
    24–25, 27, 29
diseases, 18, 27, 29

education, 20–22
entry-level jobs, 22

Food and Drug
    Administration
    (FDA), 27

food poisoning, 17,
    26–27
frozen foods, 9, 24,
    27, 29

genetic engineering,
    18, 27

internships, 21–22

labels, 5, 6, 9, 10
laboratories, 5, 12, 22

mad cow disease, 18

nanotechnology, 27,
    28
Nelson, Philip E.,
    14, 29

packaging, 5, 9, 10,
    13, 27, 28, 29
pasteurization, 10

Perchonok, Michele,
    29
proteins, 6, 14,
    18, 29

refrigeration, 5, 9, 10
research, 5, 13, 16,
    22, 27

safety, 4–5, 8, 9, 17,
    18, 26, 27
Scrimshaw, Nevin S.,
    29
shipping, 5, 9, 14, 29
storage, 9, 14, 17,
    21, 29

testing, 5, 6, 8, 13,
    14, 16, 27

United States
    Department of
    Agriculture (USDA),
    5

ABOUT THE AUTHOR

Barbara Somervill writes many books on science and the environment. Before becoming an author, she worked for a foodservice company and frequently worked with the corporate food scientist. She lives in the foothills of the Blue Ridge Mountains with her husband and faithful dog, Sydney.